Remi Oluyale

Unless otherwise indicated, all scripture quotations in this book are from the King James Version (KJV) of the Bible.

THE MAIN CAUSE OF MARITAL CONFLICTS AND THE SOLUTION
Copyright © 2004 Remi Oluyale
Second Edition 2016
ISBN: 978-37718-7-6

Printed by CreateSpace

All rights reserved. No portion of this publication may be used without the express written consent of the publisher.

CONTENTS

1. The Hydra-Headed 'Monster' 5

2. Marital Expectations 13

3. The Problem in Eden 27

4. Living Up to Expectations 39

5. Other Major Marital Expectations of a Wife 49

6. Other Major Marital Expectations of a Husband 71

7. You Can Make It 81

DEDICATION

This book is dedicated to God, the author and finisher of our faith. Wisdom and might are His. He gives wisdom to the wise and knowledge to those who have understanding. He reveals deep and secret things. He knows what is in the darkness, and light dwells with Him. Glory to His name.

I also want to acknowledge the works of Willard F. Harley in his book, 'His Needs Her Needs'. His work was very handy towards the latter part of this book. If I am judged right, I would have taken the works of Willard F Harley to the next level.[1]

1
THE HYDRA-HEADED 'MONSTER'

In marriage, conflicts are inevitable. At one time or the other, couples do have different opinions on same issues. When differences in opinions are not handled rightly, it can lead to conflicts. Conflicts are not the problems in marriage, but unresolved conflicts. To properly resolve any conflict, we need to get to the roots of the conflict. Roots are usually hidden from ordinary view. It is a common knowledge that every tree has roots even when the roots are not visible from the outside. But knowing there are roots is different from knowing what the roots are or where the roots are especially when we are talking of conflicts, any kind of conflict. The principle of resolving conflicts is the same, but we are concerned here with marital conflicts.

The Hydra-Headed 'Monster'

Is it possible to unveil the major cause of all conflicts in marriage? The problem of marital conflict is like a many-headed monster, but with one heart. The only one heart pumps blood, or call it 'fury' into all the heads. What is the heart of this monster? Many theories had been propounded by many researchers, psychologists and marriage counsellors in an attempt to discover what the main cause of marital conflicts is. Even though many of these theories are true, they are like the many heads of the same monster. In other words, they are different ways of looking at the same big problem.

If one particular head of the monster (a problem) surfaces in a marriage, and the head is cut off (problem solved), there will definitely be peace in that marriage until another 'head' of the monster surfaces. I believe a better way to deal with this 'monster' is to discover the location of the heart of the monster and aim at it with the full force of a missile in order to bring it down. Once the problematic 'heart' stops pumping, all the protruding heads die.

Having read so many books on marriage, and from my personal experience in marriage counselling, I discovered that the main culprit behind marital conflicts is unfulfilled expectations. I see unfulfilled expectations as not just one of the reasons for marital conflicts (as propounded by many

The Main Cause Of Marital Conflicts And The Solution

writers), but as the main reason for marital conflicts. It is the root reason from which other reasons stem. If marital conflict is seen as a many-headed monster, then unfulfilled expectation is the heart of the monster, pumping fury into the heads. To have a good marriage, both partners need to have their expectations met.

Expectations

Expectations are what a man or a woman hopes to get for taking a decision or for investing into a partnership. Marriage is a partnership where a man and a woman had invested their lives and means. So, the expectations are very high. Everything we do on earth is backed up with the hope of a reward. Rewards need not be only monetary. It could also be an emotional fulfilment, a place of honour or an eternal reward.

Our relationship with God as Christians is based on faith. Faith itself is established on hope and assurance. No Christian is committed to God in vain.

> *"But without faith, it is impossible to please Him, for he that cometh to God must believe that He is, and that He is a rewarder of them that diligently seek Him."*   *(Heb. 11:6)*

The Hydra-Headed 'Monster'

When we come to God, we normally expect to get some benefits from our commitments to God and His work. The word of God is full of promises. These promises have conditions for us to fulfil. For as long as we meet those conditions (our covenant commitments), it is normal for us to expect to have the promises fulfilled in our lives. Even though, sometimes, it is possible to have a wrong or an unrealistic expectation as a result of non-information (ignorance) or misinformation, there is nothing basically wrong with having expectations when we are making a business or life commitment. It should be noted therefore, that when a man and a woman come together as husband and wife, they expect to gain or benefit some things from the relationship. Sometimes, they might not be overtly conscious of this fact, but it is there lying in their minds.

Unfulfilled Expectations

A big company was recently closed down by the owners because the company was running at a loss consistently over a period of time. The owners had some expectations from the company which were not realized. At the beginning, things were OK, but later, some government policies negatively affected this company. The management of this company took a decision to close down the company as a result of unfulfilled expectations. Instead of making profits, they were

The Main Cause Of Marital Conflicts And The Solution

increasingly becoming bankrupt.

Many couples today have taken a management decision to "wind up" their relationships because of unfulfilled expectations. Many other marriages merely exist to keep the dignity of their names. Some other couples are still holding series of 'management meetings' to decide on the fate of their relationship. Meanwhile, they are only operating skeletal services in the relationships for now. The husband and wife are living just as neighbours under the same roof!

When expectations are not met, frustrations set in. Many have uttered statements like: "I am fed up with this relationship", "I just don't love her anymore", "I am simply tired of her/him", "This marriage can't just work!", "Maybe we are not meant for each other" etc. These kinds of statements are statements born out of frustrations. They show dissatisfactions with relationships. The reason for these frustrations is unfulfilled expectations.

A Chain Reaction

Frustrations eventually lead to lack of cooperation between couples. When a spouse suddenly starts becoming uncooperative with his/her partner, it is a way of saying: "Since I can't get what I expected to get from you, then you

The Hydra-Headed 'Monster'

should also not get what you expect to get from me". Actions they say, speak louder than words. Actions also provoke reactions.

Lack of cooperation will definitely lead to misunderstanding. This is because reactions are always misinterpreted. For example, a man whose wife suddenly becomes uncooperative sexually will rather think that his wife is seeing somebody else than to believe that she is merely reacting to her frustrations in the marriage. When a husband who is denied sex refuses to respond to his wife's emotional and financial needs, the wife may simply assume that the husband is no longer interested in her or even cheating on her. When reactions are misinterpreted, misunderstanding sets in.

Actions and reactions lead to misunderstandings, and eventually degenerate into crisis, which is characterized by shouting, fierce arguments and fighting. James, who doubles as a Bible study teacher and an elder in his church came to see me one early morning with a lot of worries on his face. He simply informed me that he has given his wife a condition that if she continues her unruly behaviours, he was going to divorce her. When I asked what those unruly behaviours were, he explained that his wife, Mary, had become a different woman now. She insults him, talks to him anyhow, calls him

The Main Cause Of Marital Conflicts And The Solution

names and even curses him to his face. I nearly asked if Mary had backslidden, but knowing fully well that I have only heard one half of the full story, I pleaded with James to hold his peace and give me time till the next day to come and see his wife before I know what to say.

The following day in the evening, I went to see Mary. She was already expecting me. James was also seated. Mary started narrating her own side of the story. She was also fed up with her husband. She expressed her frustrations with her husband for his insensitivity and uncontrollable anger. She related how her husband had physically abused her on several occasions. She said she can no longer tolerate being kicked left and right all the time. As far as she was concerned, it is now fire for fire or else, each one goes his/her way.

What happened to this couple is that unfulfilled expectations had degenerated into fighting. In some cases, the couples may not result to physical combat, but they know that they are having a fight. Frequent fighting eventually leads to loss of tolerance. Sister Mary could no longer tolerate her husband's uncontrolled temper and they are both looking towards the door of separation and divorce.

We can summarize how unfulfilled expectations lead to

The Hydra-Headed 'Monster'

divorce in the descending order below:

Unfulfilled expectations

Frustration

Lack of Cooperation

Misunderstanding

Fighting (Crisis)

Loss of tolerance

Separation

Divorce.

2

MARITAL EXPECTATIONS

Marital expectations can be divided into two categories. I will name them as **Individuality Expectations** and **Gender Expectations.** Individuality expectations are personal and adjustable while gender expectations are general to a particular gender and iron-cast in nature.

(1) Individuality Expectations

Husband and wife are two different individuals. They were conceived, born and brought up under different environments by different parents. They have differences in tastes and likes. No matter how compatible they appear to each other, they must still have some striking differences.

Marital Expectations

As a result of the individuality of each partner, each of them has different expectations of what they desire their spouse to be. She has her notion of whom he should be and he also has his notion of whom she should be. Their notions are as a result of the environments they both grew from. Environment and upbringing have a great influence on determining our outlook to life and preferences. Wale grew under an abusive father who would beat up his step mum at the least provocation. Wale's mum was divorced from his father and remarried to another man who is now Wale's stepfather. Wale lived in two worlds. He was with his mum and his stepdad till he was twelve years old. Then, he was moved to live with his father and his step mum. Wale's dad and mum both had anger problems. Their short marriage was explosive with violent conflicts. The marriage only managed to last for three years before it disintegrated. Wale was a baby and didn't really know how it happened between his parents before they divorced. Luckily for his mum, her present husband is cool headed and can manage the anger of his wife without violent conflicts. Somehow, they are tagging along in their marriage. At first, it was a shock for Wale seeing his dad beating his step mum. Later, he became used to it and with some 'coaching' from his dad; he believed that women usually need to be beaten back into their senses.

The Main Cause Of Marital Conflicts And The Solution

Now in adult life, Wale is married and there is trouble brewing in his marriage. They did not really court for a sufficient time before they got married. Tina became pregnant and they had to hurriedly arrange the marriage. Tina's father never raised his hands against her mum. They used to have quarrels, but it never degenerated to the level of physical combat. Wale has taken after his dad! Tina is in trouble! If only she has not gotten pregnant and had enough time to assess Wale, she would not have married him. Eventually, she discovered that Wale had issues with his temper. For this marriage not to end in a divorce, Wale needs to unlearn and relearn, while Tina needs to make adjustments in her mind of what to expect from her husband. The reality is that they both need to agree to make some adjustments in their individual lifestyles and expectations from each other. They now go to church and that is helping a great deal.

A woman who grew in a peaceful home where both parents loved each other and cared for their children would have been dreaming of marrying a man who would do everything just like her father. Another woman who grew under an irresponsible and unfaithful father, who always cursed and lied, would have unconsciously made up her mind that all men are irresponsible. It will be difficult for her to trust her husband. A man whose mother was a great cook would expect

Marital Expectations

a wife who can cook just like his mother.

When these individuality expectations are not met, it leads to the comparison syndrome which eventually results in frustrations. Both partners become frustrated over time and actions start leading to reactions. In order to save yourself from unnecessary frustrations and conflicts in marriage, you must divorce your personal feelings of what you want your spouse to be from what your spouse really is. Know that your spouse is a distinct individual. He or she is not like your parents or whosoever brought you up. Look at him/her differently from the others you came across on your way to growing up. Your husband is not a repetition of your generous uncle or brutal father. Your husband is not that man that raped you or your first boy friend that jilted you. Your wife is not a replica of your mother. They may have some similarities, but they are never the same. She is not your quiet and gentle sister you grew up with, neither is she the girl that nearly cost you your life some years ago before you met your wife.

Don't punish your spouse for the sins others committed against you. Don't compare your spouse with the values you've seen in others. Your spouse has other values that are absent in those others you earlier admired.

The Main Cause Of Marital Conflicts And The Solution

Your spouse is a new person in your life for you to discover. Relate with your spouse on his/her merit, not on the merit of others whom he/she might even never have met. Marriage is a journey of discovery which never ends until one of the partners dies or the marriage is broken.

Individuality expectations sometimes are unrealistic and selfish. Don't seek only for what you can get. Also seek for what you can give. There is excitement in discoveries. Try to discover your spouse to know who your spouse really is, so that you can know what is realistic to expect from him/her and thereby be content. Godliness with contentment is great gain (I Tim.6:6). When what you are passionate about is not in your spouse, you can discuss it or seek for counselling so you can both make adjustments in your lifestyles and expectations and not just keep chasing shadows. Adjustments can be made to your personal expectations where those expectations cannot be realistically met in your marriage. Conflicts at any level can never be truly resolved without both sides making a shift, no matter how little, from their positions. The model of resolving conflicts in marriage is a principle that can be applied in the larger society i.e. workplace, associations, communities and nations.

(2) Gender Expectations

God created men and women differently. Men and women are completely different physically, mentally and emotionally. As a result of gender differences, there are some marital

Marital Expectations

expectations that are common in order of priority to men and some that are common in order of priority to women. These marital expectations are not a matter of individuality but of gender. A misunderstanding of this kind of expectations and how to fulfil them is the root cause of multiple divorce rates in the world today. There are some traits that are common to all women that a man compulsorily needs to understand in order to relate with any woman on earth. There are also some traits that are common to all men that a woman compulsorily needs to understand in order to relate with any man on earth. Unlike individuality expectations, gender expectations cannot be adjusted or changed.

A Striking Difference

If all husbands are to write all they expect from their wives and all wives are to write all they expect from their husbands, we will find out that there would be some similarities and some differences in what they would write. The common factor between men and women is the human nature. The difference is the gender.

In carefully examining the two lists presented by husbands and wives, a striking difference would be noticed. The striking difference between men and women in marital expectations is **PRIORITY.**

The Main Cause Of Marital Conflicts And The Solution

Priority differs between genders in almost everything and marriage is not an exception. What tops the list of a man's expectations in marriage is radically different from what tops the list of a woman's expectations.

The Big Mistake Couples Make

There is a string of error that if not removed from a relationship can easily and quickly pull down any marriage. This error is the big mistake of unconsciously expecting that what is a priority to you should also be a priority to your spouse. This pattern of thinking stems from the human nature of tending to generalize a personal feeling. For example, if a man has high temperature as a result of fever, he feels may be everybody is also feeling the same way he is feeling. It takes a conscious mental effort to inform oneself that not all personal feelings are general. Sometimes, you may need to ask your neighbour how he/she feels so that you can be sure nobody else is experiencing the high body temperature you are battling with.

Many times, husbands expect their wives to feel and think the same way they do. Wives also many times erroneously get disappointed that their husbands are not giving the same priorities to things they hold in high esteem. Men and women see things differently. What is of a high priority to a man is not necessarily of a high priority to a woman. Husbands and

Marital Expectations

wives need to learn this truth early enough in marriage. Otherwise, they will only be chasing shadows and can soon get frustrated with each other.

Importance of Priority

It is very wise to understand the importance of priority. Economists say human wants are unlimited but the resources are limited. Since resources are limited, man needs to list his wants in order of importance. The most important need comes first and the others follow, depending on how important they are. The first item on the scale of preference becomes a priority. This means no matter how little the resources are, the priority item on the list must first be attended to before any other item. Even if all other items are going to wait, the priority item cannot wait. It also means that until the priority item is taken care of, it is assumed nothing has been done. For example, the priority of a rational student for attending a higher institution is to earn a degree. Whatever is achieved in that school at the end of the day is nothing without the degree.

Marital Priorities

Having understood what a priority is, marital priorities therefore, are those marital expectations that top the lists of husbands and wives. In my marriage seminars, I usually ask the women to give me a list of what they expect from their

The Main Cause Of Marital Conflicts And The Solution

husbands. There is usually a very long list. The men on the other hand usually give a shorter list. Many times the lists do have some similarities, but the emphasis of the women is usually different from where the men lay their emphasis.

My Discovery

If we are to arrange men's marital expectations in a scale of preference, top on the list is going to be boldly written: SEXUAL FULFILLMENT. (Most writers and researchers agree on this). On the other hand, if we are to arrange women's marital expectations in a scale of preference, top on the list is going to be boldly written: TALKING TOGETHER (i.e. 'conversation' or broadly put, 'communication'). Contrary to general belief that a woman's number one need is affection, I discovered that every woman's greatest marital need or expectation is having a heartfelt conversation with her husband. I am aware that this is a complete departure from the norm. It has been taught over the years by everybody that affection tops the priority list of a woman. This is the very reason why in spite of all the affectionate words, the woman is still unfulfilled.

It is important to accurately diagnose a situation or an illness before an effective solution or treatment can be administered. According to Wikipedia, 'Diagnosis is the identification of

Marital Expectations

the nature and cause of a certain phenomenon'. There is a need to rightly identify the nature and cause of marital disharmony so that an effective treatment can be administered. Where there is a misdiagnosis, there will also be a flaw in treatment. There is no end to knowledge and discoveries. With this discovery, I believe marriage counsellors may now be able to proffer better solutions to the issue of 'unknown' causes of marital conflicts that had been tearing marriages into shreds all over the world. Marriage therapists can now see 'Conversation' as a priority need for women in marriage, thereby encouraging husbands to prioritise sitting down and talking with their wives above giving of affection.

What gives the woman the same level of fulfilment the man has in sexual fulfilment is not affection at all. It is rather, a heartfelt conversation. Sexual intercourse naturally originates from the man. Affection also originates from the man. I discovered that whatever would give the woman the peak of marital satisfaction must be something that originates from the woman. The man should not be the initiator of what gives him maximum fulfilment in marriage and at the same time, also be the initiator of what gives the woman maximum fulfilment in marriage. A woman is not a dud. She intuitively longs for what gives her relieve, satisfaction and fulfilment (which is conversation), even though she has been schooled to

The Main Cause Of Marital Conflicts And The Solution

accept that affection should be her number one marital need. Each one knows where he or she feels hunger. Inevitably, the woman also has something to offer. It is not only about the man and what he does or gets. It is rather, about the woman and the man. It is about what they both do and get which can be described as fulfilment or the peak of their excitement and happiness for being together as husband and wife. Each gender knows what gives him/her the maximum fulfilment and seeks to have it by initiating steps in that direction. Hence, the man initiates sex, the woman initiates conversation.

If affection indeed is the woman's number one marital need, it then means she can't initiate what she longs for, but only have to wait for the man to remember what she needs and give it to her. This does not sound logical enough, as human beings generally seek and initiate steps in the direction of whatever gives them fulfilment in life. Even babies initiate steps toward what they desire to have. A baby can lift up her hands toward an adult when she wishes to be carried by the adult. She doesn't just sit down there, expecting the adult to intuitively know what she desires. When the baby is hungry and needs to eat, he cries and longs for the food until it is provided. A woman naturally knows what her priority need is and she intuitively longs and takes steps toward meeting that need even when she has been tutored to believe that need is something else. Hence, a woman constantly initiates steps toward conversation and feels highly embarrassed, depressed, unrelieved, dissatisfied and unfulfilled when she is denied of it.

Marital Expectations

Affectionate words or actions are those little sweet words or actions originating from a man, which means so much to a woman emotionally. Every woman has needs for affection, but conversation as we are going to see is of a higher priority to any woman even when a woman does not know it as a fact. There is a law or a principle I called 'the principle of pouring'. We will soon get into that.

Understandably, a woman's mind had been programmed with the information that affection is her priority or number one need in marriage because this had been the general believe in marriage counseling. In my marriage seminars, by the time I finish speaking on this topic, I leave the women themselves to judge. To many women, it's like a veil lifting off their eyes. They usually agree that my discovery is accurate and that if men could heed to my advice, they as women would have less emotional stress which will go a long way in reducing conflicts in marriage generally. The priority need of the woman can now also be put in its proper place and met accordingly. Now there can be true peace and fulfilment on both sides. So, what tops the list of a man's marital expectation is 'sexual fulfilment', while what tops the list of a woman's marital expectation is now discovered to be 'conversation fulfilment'. Conversation is under communication, so we could also say 'communication

The Main Cause Of Marital Conflicts And The Solution

fulfilment', but communication is broad and wide. We'll miss the point if we use the words: 'communication fulfilment'. So, it is more appropriate here to use the words 'conversation fulfilment'. However, sometimes, the words: 'conversation' and 'communication' can still be used interchangeably. It is very important to get this straight, so that couples would know how to appropriately dissipate their time and energy in building their relationship. It is only when priority needs are fully met that meeting other needs could make any meaning! Meaning: if indeed, conversation is the woman's priority need, no woman can get fulfilled in her marriage until her conversation need is met. Whatever her husband does to please her without first and foremost taking care of this priority need in her life would mean little or nothing.

The wife is always eager to relate all that happened during the day on sighting her husband. The husband on the other hand is not particularly interested in talking, but can easily be turned on for sex by just seeing and admiring his wife. Conscious steps need to be taken by couples to get out of their gender boxes and reach out to meet their partner's marital needs for peace to reign in their relationship. This problem had been from the beginning of creation as we are going to see in the Garden of Eden.

3
THE PROBLEM IN EDEN

The Problem In Eden

"Now the serpent was more subtle than any beast of the field which the Lord God had made. And he said unto the woman Yea, hath God said, Ye shall not eat of every tree of the garden? And the woman said unto the serpent, we may eat of the fruit of the trees of the garden. But of the fruit of the tree which is in the midst of the garden, God hath said, ye shall not eat of it,

The Problem In Eden

neither shall ye touch it, lest ye die."
(Gen.3:1-3)

As we entered the new millennium in year 2000, one cool evening, I just finished a counseling session and I began to meditate. Then, just in a flash, the Spirit of God took me (in the spirit) to the Garden of Eden. God made me to see by revelation, the reason why the first marriage failed. I saw that this is still the major reason why several marriages are failing today. Adam and Eve did not physically separate or divorce as we have it done today because it was only the two of them in the whole earth. Eve was tempted by the serpent, fell for the temptation and ate the forbidden fruit. She gave the fruit to her husband who also ate and they both fell from grace and fellowship with God. If Eve was confused about what God said concerning the forbidden fruit, what of Adam? Was he also confused and deceived? Was it love that made him follow Eve in the sin or was it a counter sin because he felt cheated by his wife's romance with the serpent as some spouses are still tempted to do today? Well, your guess is as good as mine!

I saw that the first marriage failed in Eden because Adam refused to give enough attention to his wife. Adam was very busy with the assignment of keeping the garden. Eve had expected Adam to spend enough time with her regularly so

The Main Cause Of Marital Conflicts And The Solution

that she can pour out her heart into him and have good times to gist. On the contrary, Adam was very 'hard working'. He had no time to spare for the "bone of his bones and flesh of his flesh". Adam refused to communicate well with Eve.

Satan had been before Eden. When he saw what God did in Eden, he became envious and jealous of Adam and Eve. Each day as he saw them relate with each other and with God, he was sad and dejected (he is still sad and dejected at every working marriage till today!). Satan had cunningly been looking for a way to enter the Garden of Eden and cause confusion. For as long as Adam and Eve were firmly knitted together, doing the work of keeping the garden, walking around together and talking, Satan had no way. The devil can patiently wait in anticipation of an opportune time! After a while, Satan began to notice a crack in the fence. There was a loophole in the marriage of Adam and Eve. He saw Adam becoming 'very' busy and Eve becoming much neglected.

Something was crying in Eve for fulfilment. Eve needed somebody to talk to! Eve was feeling lonely while Adam was busy enjoying his work. Eve's heart was full. She wished she had enough attention from her husband, so she could pour her heart into him. Adam the workaholic! A man not given to many words. He needed to work hard because the garden was

The Problem In Eden

big and so many things were calling for attention. He wished Eve could understand and just summarize whatever was bothering her like he would do. Frustrated, Eve decided to keep so many things bothering her to herself.

As soon as Satan perceived a communication gap between this divinely-celebrated couple, he knew it was time to strike. Satan cunningly took advantage of Eve's vulnerability at this time. He came to Eve as a friend that is ready to talk and listen. Please note here that he did not come as 'Satan'. He came as a friend! He came with a voice of familiarity: **"Ye, hath God said..."** It was like saying: *"Hi Eve, can we talk about all those things God said?"* Eve's eyes brightened up. She could not help but respond courteously. Eve started pouring her heart and was really enjoying the discussion. She was feeling relieved of the burden in her heart as she kept pouring and pouring. As she was feeling relieved, she was also getting satisfied and fulfilled, enjoying the company. Before she knew what was happening, the serpent had confused her, made her to doubt what God really said and seeing the serpent as a "caring" being, she took the forbidden fruit and ate.

Eve was easily lured by the serpent because she had been looking for somebody she can really gist with. Adam was too busy for Eve, so the marriage fell. If you don't have time for

The Main Cause Of Marital Conflicts And The Solution

your wife, the serpent has all the time and is willing. Your wife becomes vulnerable when she is starved of fellowship with you.

Men usually do think that once they are able to provide money and comfort in their homes, their wives are already fully taken care of. This is an erroneous believe. Stories had been told of women who though had every material comfort in the home, still got frustrated and moved out with less privileged men who have the time to listen and fellowship with them. Many marriages today, are still suffering what Adam and Eve suffered in the Garden of Eden. That is why many homes are failing, and divorce rate is on the increase. Just as sexual fulfilment is a priority need to the male gender, so is conversation a priority need to the female gender.

It is a Matter of Pouring

I discovered this principle I tag: **"The principle of pouring"**. Through inspiration, I discovered that it is this principle of pouring that actually determines what gives the peak of marital satisfaction, relief, and fulfilment to either the husband or wife in a marriage setting.

Men who don't have time for their wives often wonder why their wives frequently cook up excuses to avoid sexual

The Problem In Eden

intimacy. The reason is because whosoever allows a woman to pour her heart into him is the person the woman will unconsciously be ready to receive into herself. The woman is loaded in her heart while the man is loaded in his loins. Pouring brings a lot of relief, satisfaction and fulfilment. If a man allows a woman to pour her heart into him, the woman will also allow the man to pour his loins into her. The woman is naturally a responder. Unconsciously, a woman finds herself responding to any man who meets this priority need in her life. The man even needs not be her husband. The man needs not be more educated, richer, more handsome or more popular than her husband. It might be that seemingly harmless Mr. Satan lurking in the corner, always waiting patiently and looking for an opportunity to take over the discussion with the woman!

This explains why neglected wives easily fall preys to adultery. And annoyingly to the men-folk, such women most of the time fall for men who may not be as highly placed in the society as their husbands, but have the time to sit down for her to pour her heart into him. For the man to always be there for her, she is ready and willing to do anything including sleeping with him. What actually happens is that when a woman pours her heart into a man consistently through conversation, she feels a part of her is already in that man. She feels already

The Main Cause Of Marital Conflicts And The Solution

bonded to him emotionally and might unconsciously feel unjustified to say no if the man asks her or makes sexual moves towards her. We can now understand why it was difficult for Eve to say no to the serpent! The same way, a man knows and feels a part of him is already deposited into a woman after he had poured himself into her through sexual intercourse. He knows something is already connecting them. He starts having a soft spot for the woman.

Pouring brings relief, fulfilment and satisfaction. A woman gets all these things when she has been allowed to pour her heart into the man who is the love of her life. A man also gets all these things after a fulfilling sexual intercourse with his darling. For a man, adultery could be a habit, but for a woman, adultery is usually a way of meeting a need. Except for women who are possessed with the spirit of lust, or are on a satanic mission against men through sex, a woman will normally be faithful to her husband if her priority need is met in her marriage. She will always be looking forward to being together so she can ask questions that are bothering her and do her pouring with the love of her life who will listen to her and attend to her worries. Couples should note that we are talking of these needs as priority needs. This means there are no alternatives to fulfilling such, if there is going to be peace in any marriage. These priority needs are gender based and the

The Problem In Eden

truth about gender based needs is that you will find them present in any member of the gender. Gender based 'problems' have no solution because they are really not 'problems', but nature. It is a take it or leave it scenario. Understanding and preparation to meet those needs are the only constructive way out. So, it is not a matter of individuality but of gender. The uncomfortable truth is: gender priority needs must be met somehow. It's either they are met within marriage (which is preferable), or they are met outside marriage (which leads to trouble). It takes a high level of spirituality and self denial for a partner whose priority need is not effectively met in his/her marriage to still be faithful to his/her spouse. Couples need to start conditioning and positioning their minds to be there for each other to be fulfilled and happy. They need not tempt each other to seek for fulfilment outside their marriage.

'Relief' is actually a result of 'pouring', something leaving your body or mind, bringing a refreshing feeling and lightness. So, the process that can bring true relief to a wife is when she pours her heart in conversation. For the husband, it is when he pours his loins through sex. The problem here is that men and women see sex and conversation from two different and distinct points of view. This leads us to the paradoxes:

The Main Cause Of Marital Conflicts And The Solution

The Paradoxes

Paradox 1
Since sex is a priority expectation to a man, it then follows that what a man enjoys most with his wife is having sexual intercourse. Since communication is a priority expectation to a woman, it then follows that what a woman enjoys most with her husband is having an heartfelt conversation.

Paradox 2
A man is easily frustrated when his wife refuses him 'sex'. A woman is easily frustrated when her husband refuses her 'talk'.

Paradox 3
A man enjoys sex the same way a woman enjoys conversation. A woman enjoys conversation the same way a man enjoys sex.

Paradox 4
The peak of marital satisfaction for a man happens during sexual intercourse. The peak of marital satisfaction for a woman happens during talking and chatting with her husband.

The Problem In Eden

Paradox 5

After sex, a man feels relieved, satisfied and lighter in his body. After a heartfelt conversation, a woman feels relieved, satisfied and lighter in her heart.

Paradox 6

The man mostly initiates sex because that is his priority need. The woman mostly initiates conversation because that is her priority need.

Paradox 7

During conversation, a woman transfers the burdens in her heart to her husband and expects him to figure out the solutions for her. As soon as she is through, the problems become her husband's. During sex, a man transfers the burdens in his loins (semen) into his wife and expects her to handle the remaining process of producing a baby. As soon as he is through, the remaining process of producing a baby becomes his wife's.

Paradox 8

The priority expectation of a woman from her husband is not sex. The priority expectation of a man from his wife is not talking.

The Main Cause Of Marital Conflicts And The Solution

Paradox 9

A man cannot change the nature of his wife from being a woman. A woman cannot change the nature of her husband from being a man.

Understanding Is Needed

Men and women should study and learn how to relate with their marriage partners. The way a man expects to be loved is completely different from the way a woman expects to be loved. When a man tries to love his wife the way he expects his wife to love him, the wife sees no love and absolutely feels unloved. When a woman also tries to love her husband the way she expects her husband to love her, the husband sees no love and absolutely feels unloved. Every man seeks for a woman who will be passionately in love with him, in whom he can consistently pour his loins through sexual intercourse. The same way, every woman seeks for a man who will be passionately in love with her, in whom she can consistently pour her heart through conversation. Couples should understand each other's 'very important' or priority needs and be positioned to meet those needs.

4
LIVING UP TO EXPECTATIONS

Living Up To Expectations

My advice to couples is to try as much as possible to live up to the expectations of their partners. True love must mean love to the recipient. If the way you have loved your spouse never meant love to him/her, then you do not yet love.

Since the priority expectation of a man from his wife is sexual fulfilment, a woman who is using sex as a weapon of war against her husband is only tearing down her marriage with her own hands.

Living Up To Expectations

"Every wise woman builds her house but the foolish plucketh it down with her hands."   *(Prov. 14:1)*

Sexual fulfilment to a man is not just something he likes to have. It is a priority need that he expects would be rightly and legally met in his life by getting married. The purpose of marriage for a man is not limited to sex. Nevertheless, sexual fulfilment remains a priority to all men in marriage. If a man is not sexually fulfilled with his wife, nothing else can work in that relationship. It is easier for other things to work well once there is sexual fulfilment.

On the other hand, communication fulfilment to a woman is not just something she likes to have. It is a priority need she expects would be rightly and legally met in her life by getting married. The purpose of marriage for a woman is not limited to communication. Nevertheless, I have discovered that communication remains a priority to all women in marriage. If a woman is not conversationally fulfilled with her husband, nothing else can work in that relationship. It is easier for other things to work well once there is conversation fulfilment.

An absentee husband can never make his wife happy. Women don't marry properties. They marry husbands! I have never heard of a woman who is fulfilled as a wife, whose husband

The Main Cause Of Marital Conflicts And The Solution

has no quality time to spend with her. When a man tells his wife to shut up, what the wife hears is "you are not important" or "I hate you". However, when a man listens to and talks with his wife, the wife feels important and loved. She feels relieved that she has poured out her heart. She is much more ready to listen to what the husband also has to 'say'.

My Recommendations

After a day's work, husband and wife return home, the children and visitors are cared for, supper is served and it's time to retire into the bedroom. Since morning when each left for the day's assignments, they are just coming back together, only the two of them as husband and wife. At this moment, the foremost thing on the mind of the wife is to relate all that happened during the day and hear her husband's version of how the day had been. The first thing on her mind at this moment is not sex.

As the wife tries to undress and put on her night gown or just briskly combs her hair, her husband's mind is already set for sex. The husband is not really interested in talking and chatting as such.

Quality Conversation

At this point, I recommend that the man exercises some

Living Up To Expectations

restraints and first take time to listen to his wife. While listening, he should pay attention to his wife. A man who is reading newspapers or watching television cannot say he is listening to his wife. Listening has to do with giving attention. The best way to listen to your wife is to close the newspaper and focus your attention on her. Let her see that nothing is sharing your attention with her. Let her know she is more important than the television set or the newspaper. Let her see that apart from God in your life, she is number one. Listen to her. If she has any question about which fruit God has forbidden in the garden of your marriage, clarify it to her. If you don't, remember the Garden of Eden! Answer her questions. Understand her feelings. Don't shout her down or laugh at the kind of questions she is asking. That is why you are her husband and talk-mate. Encourage her and let her hear from you that everything shall be alright. Share your own experience of the day as briefly as you can. Give her a peep into your day too. By this time, she is fully yours for the night! Now, she is vulnerable to you. She has really enjoyed herself. You may now go ahead and enjoy yourself too.

Are Men Also Talkative?

Is it true that men don't like to talk? I don't think so. It is not true that men don't talk! Men talk a great deal with their friends on topics of interest to them, i.e. football, movies,

The Main Cause Of Marital Conflicts And The Solution

wars etc. Sometimes, you see men talking for hours with their friends, just chatting and jumping from one topic to the other. Something common to friends is that they spend quality time together. A man should therefore make his wife his best friend and make plans to spend quality time with her.

It is culture (especially polygamy and male-chauvinism) that has programmed the minds of men to think that chatting with a woman is unmanly. Under polygamy, since a man can have so many wives, he must not be seen talking too much with any of them. Otherwise, the other wives will become jealous. In order to avoid troubles among the wives, it is assumed that it is better never to talk intimately with any of them. Even though polygamy is already becoming old fashioned, most men from the parts of the world where polygamy is allowed have the background of such a family. Unconsciously, they already erroneously picked it up from their fathers that talking and chatting with a woman is unmanly.

In the western world where polygamy is not fashionable, serial marriage has been substituted. Most of the men are chauvinistic and only want to do things that are masculine, hard and macho! They prefer to talk endlessly with their friends on topics like sports, cars, scientific breakthroughs and so on. Sitting down for some minutes and talking with

Living Up To Expectations

their wives on 'trivial' things for them is unmanly and a waste of precious time.

Any man who desires a good marriage should be ready to make simple adjustments early enough in marriage. Marriage is about two different people blending together. Both must adjust if they are committed to making their marriage a success. It is difficult to make a success out of a venture you really don't have time for. Men should make out time to sit down with their wives and talk. The bottom line is: If a woman does not consciously and intentionally set out to meet her husband's need for sexual fulfilment, she can never have peace with her husband no matter what other needs she is meeting in her husband's life. The same way, if a man does not consciously and intentionally set out to meet his wife's need for conversation, he can never have peace with his wife, no matter what other needs he is meeting in his wife's life. Selah.

After your wife has poured out her heart into you, she becomes fulfilled and satisfied with your presence. She then becomes very vulnerable to your advances. She becomes romantic herself. She feels relieved from the stress of the day and is ready to receive you into her arms in love.

This problem is practically the same with all men all over the

The Main Cause Of Marital Conflicts And The Solution

world. It is a satanic plot from the beginning to always frustrate the woman and make her vulnerable to the serpent's advances. This mind-set is contrary to God's intentions for marriage. A man's best friend should be his wife. A woman's best friend should also be her husband. A man should start practicing how to listen and talk with his wife. After some time, the man will get used to it and start enjoying it. Women should also make up their minds to always give their husband the best treat on the bed. This is the way of peace.

The Art of Love Making

Making love is an art that men and women need to learn. A man is made ready and prepared for sex by sight. A woman is not prepared for sex by merely seeing her husband. A woman is stirred up for sexual intercourse by romance. For this reason, a man needs to carry his wife along sexually by spending enough time in romance in order to arouse and make her ready for him. When a woman is aroused, she becomes wet and lubricated. The lubrication helps the sexual act to run smoothly. When a woman is not well lubricated and the man comes in, friction occurs and the woman is bruised. A constantly sexually bruised woman would soon associate sex with pain and later becomes frigid. Such women don't hide their hatred for sex.

Living Up To Expectations

Another area a man needs to master in sex is taking his wife to orgasm. Many men don't even know that a woman can attain orgasm. The man necessarily reaches orgasm (the peak of sexual satisfaction) when he ejaculates. A woman does not necessarily reach orgasm when her husband ejaculates. The man should learn how to slow down for his wife to catch up with his speed and gradually take her to orgasm before he finally ejaculates. It is possible for a woman to reach orgasm more than once in just one sexual act.

A woman who does not have the experience of orgasm would have only felt used. She feels woken up for nothing. Probably at the time she was just getting ready in her body for sex, the man is already at the climax, reaches orgasm and ejaculates. The show is suddenly over just at the time she is ready to enjoy the show. Such experiences lead to sexual frustration, frigidity and hatred for sex.

Men should be gentle with their wives when it comes to sex. The woman's mind is involved in sex. So, a man should take time to prepare his wife's mind for sex by being romantic in his utterances and acts. A man should also spend enough time in romance to make sure his wife is fully woken up and well lubricated for sex before penetration.

The Main Cause Of Marital Conflicts And The Solution

A woman should cooperate in bed with her husband. Sex should not be used as a weapon to get back at him. Sex is a consummation of the marital union and should be seen as holy and sacred. Lack of conjugation can nullify a marriage. A woman should respond and participate in the sexual act. She should not just "allow him to do his thing". She should rather cooperate and participate for their mutual enjoyment. Women do enjoy sex too, especially when their husband is gentle, patient and knowledgeable about how to take them to orgasm.

There are so many books already written basically on the subject of sex by anointed men and women of God. I advice couples who are having sexually related problems in their marriage to avail themselves of the opportunities of these books. Counselling can also be sought from Godly counsellors.

When the priority needs or expectations are met in marriage, it becomes easier for other expectations to be met. These expectations are needs that couples expect to be met in their marriages. The difference between the priority needs and other marital needs is that priority needs are to be met first and foremost before meeting other needs can count in the heart of your partner. Talking about not putting the cart before the horses, priority needs (sexual fulfilment and conversation)

Living Up To Expectations

are the horses while other marital needs are in the 'cart'. The problem with the general notion of making affection as the priority need of the woman has been the problem of putting the cart before the horses. This means that no matter how much the show of affection from the husband, if the wife has nowhere in him to effectively pour her heart, she will still remain frustrated, unrelieved, unsatisfied and unfulfilled.

However, the responsibility of meeting each other's needs does not stop at meeting only the priority needs. The idea is that meeting the priority needs makes it easier and reasonable for other needs to be met.

5
OTHER MAJOR MARITAL NEEDS OF A WIFE

Other major marital expectations of a wife are:

Affection
Appreciation
Security
Family commitment.

1. Affection
Next to communication is the need for affection in the heart of every woman. Affection has to do with some little things a man can do or say that means so much deeply and emotionally

Other Major Marital Needs Of A Wife

to a woman. A woman's day can be made by just a show of affection. Every woman needs affection and expects this need to be met by her husband. Remember, this is a gender need and it must be met. Gender needs are not negotiable.

Many men wrongly confuse the need for affection in a woman for her desire for sex. When a woman hugs a man, she is not necessarily asking for sex. She just wants to be held gently for some moments. An additional kiss or a peck will mean so much to her emotionally than a hurried sexual intercourse at such moments.

Nonsexual touches are great ways of showing affection to a woman. A lot of women receive more affection outside than they receive at home. Any woman can easily be overtaken by an excessive show of affection. Men should therefore know their limits when it comes to showing affection to a woman outside their marriage. A woman is always looking forward to being in the presence of somebody who showers affection on her. Many had fallen into adultery that way.

Other ways to show affection include writing short notes and placing them where she will easily see them. Such short notes reading 'you are the best' or a short passionate poem about her beauty can fill her day with excitements. If she sees the note

The Main Cause Of Marital Conflicts And The Solution

just before retiring into the bedroom, that night could just be your greatest night ever.

You can also show her affection by giving flowers, cards, holding her hands softly on a stroll, taking her out for dinner, offering her an helping hand at home, calling her on phone at midday just to tell her some sweet words, opening the door of the car for her, etc. If a husband fulfils his wife's need for affection at home, whatever affection she gets outside will not mean so much to her. On the other hand, a woman who is thirsty, hungry and famished for just a few sweet words from her husband can easily fall for anything outside. Such a woman will need a very strong will and determination not to give-in to an affectionate outsider.

Some men were not brought up affectionately. They are not used to being caressed, hugged and called nice names. However, they knew their parents loved them, provided for their needs and cared for them. Some other men were not even brought up by their parents, especially, their mothers. Such men never experienced what affection is. They therefore don't believe a show of affection is anything to bother about. Such men need to consciously and willingly come out of the box they've found themselves. If the wife happens to be someone who had enjoyed pampering all her life, there is no

Other Major Marital Needs Of A Wife

way she will believe that her unaffectionate husband loves her. Such men need to learn how to show affection and make some behavioural adjustments in their marriage to prevent a big crisis brewing. A woman should not be expected to adjust to living in her marriage without receiving affection. This is looking for trouble! Gender needs are innate. It is common to every member of that gender. There are no other ways of resolving gender needs other than to understand and meet them. Therefore, it is the husband that should make the adjustment and learn how to show affection to his darling wife.

Every man can learn how to show affection to his wife through practise. Enjoying a happy and a successful home requires hard work. Any man who is determined and committed can do it. An African adage says: "Little by little, a monkey learns how to jump from trees to trees without falling". Every man can do it!

WHAT A WIFE IS ASKING FOR:
There are three major things she is saying through her gender need for affection:

1. Notice me: Every wife wants her husband to notice her. When she puts on a beautiful dress, she is waiting for his

The Main Cause Of Marital Conflicts And The Solution

comments. She won't tell him in words like "hey, I'm waiting for your comments", but in her heart, that is what she is saying. If her husband refuses to notice her and comment nicely, she is put down and disappointed. But if he says something like: "wao! This is nice on you", she is elated. She feels good about herself and her husband. An emotional need is met. So, men should take time to notice her. Notice her new hairstyle. Don't complain about how much time she spent in the saloon. Appreciate her efforts to looking beautiful and make nice comments. When she is not feeling fine, she wants you to notice. She is waiting for you to come close and empathise with her. She wants you to hold her and assure her she will be alright. She wants you to care for her by asking if she has taken medications. Women expect their husbands to be 'mind readers'. So, she is always saying something in her heart and expects her lover to 'hear'. She is always saying in her heart: Notice me!

2. Express your feelings towards me.
Verbal expressions are very important to women. She is saying (in her mind) to her husband, tell me what you feel about me. If you love me, say it. Let me hear it from your mouth that you love me. Don't just say it in your mind, verbalize it. Express your love verbally. Say it over and over again. I can't be tired of hearing you saying "I love you

Other Major Marital Needs Of A Wife

sweetie". Don't tell me you said it yesterday, I want to hear it again today! When I hear you say it that is when I am assured of your love. Tell me I'm beautiful. Tell me I'm the center of your universe. Tell me how important I am to you. Also speak well about me behind my back. I want to hear people tell me how you speak nicely about me to them.

3. Touch me

Stretch your hand towards me and hold me. Hug me. Put your hands around my shoulders even before your friends and family members. Hold me close to yourself. Hold my hands when walking together. Be proud of me and let the whole neighbourhood know that I am your wife.

So, to effectively show affection, husbands should constantly notice, verbally express their love and regularly touch their wife. If a man understands what affection does to a woman, he will be careful on how he showers it on a woman that is not his wife. He would rather reserve his energy to be affectionate to constantly sweep his wife off her feet by his excessive show of affection to meet his wife's gender based emotional need.

Should a wife show affection to her husband?

Do men also have need for affection? Oh yes, they do. The only difference is that affection is not a major or a priority

The Main Cause Of Marital Conflicts And The Solution

need for men. The male gender has different items on his priority list. Affection is on men's list, but it does not make the first five items. Men enjoy affection but women cannot do without it.

Why a husband won't show affection?
Where should we check if a husband won't notice his wife, verbally express his love to his wife or touch her affectionately? What could be the problem? Why would affection disappear in a marriage?

1. Check his background: How did he grow up? Has he learned how to show affection while growing up? As we discussed earlier, if this is the problem, the man should take conscious steps to learn how to show affection through practise. He can make a list of what to say to his wife at different times and commit himself to saying them. With time, he will get used to it. With determination and commitment, any feat can be accomplished.

2. Check his work: Some jobs are so demanding that the man has little time left for romance. Some men are constantly travelling on official duties and majorly preoccupied with their jobs. Any married man with a highly demanding job needs to apply wisdom and order his priorities right. A

Other Major Marital Needs Of A Wife

married man should create time to attend to the needs of his wife, no matter what! "My job is highly demanding" is not an excuse not to call, send email, tweets, notice her, remember her birthday or hug her. Whatever little time is left for the family should be judiciously spent to make up for times you are not available.

3. Check his finance: When a man is undergoing a serious financial stress and can't meet his financial obligations, he may not be very excited about himself. This situation may also affect his responses to his wife and children. A man that is undergoing serious financial difficulties needs a lot of encouragement and assurance from his wife. His wife can do a lot to help him see the situation in a better perspective. Times and seasons do change. The man can also help himself by encouraging himself in the Lord his God if he has a relationship with God. He should be conscious of the important people in his life and do his best to be there for them emotionally. He should also trust God for a turnaround in his finances.

4. Check his wife: Sometimes, a woman can contribute to her husband's lack of interest in relating affectionately with her. A wife who does not care about the way she dresses will surely not get nice comments about her look. It is important for a

The Main Cause Of Marital Conflicts And The Solution

woman to dress nicely in a way her husband will admire.

A wife's constant nagging, criticisms, insults and frequent usage of demeaning words on her husband will push the man away from her physically and emotionally. Under such circumstances, affectionate words cannot flow. There must be boundaries in marriage relationships. No matter what, some boundaries should not be broken. Using demeaning words on each other will not help any relationship.

5. Check his secret life: A man who is cheating on his wife or addicted to porn may be lacking in meeting his wife's emotional need for affection. The evil some men do in the secret will negatively impact on their marriage in the open. Even when the secret is still hidden, the negative effect cannot be hidden. There will be some traces of a change in behaviour and intimacy with his wife. Women are very sensitive and can easily pick it when something is not sitting right in their husband's behaviour.

Men who abuse drugs and alcohol are usually abusive towards their wife. This is because they are always under influence and can't think straight for themselves. Such men don't have time for affection. To break the yoke of addiction to immorality and substance abuse, Jesus is the answer.

Other Major Marital Needs Of A Wife

Salvation in Christ brings a total change. *"When a man is in Christ, he is a new creation, old things are passed away, behold, all things are become new"*. (II Cor. 5:17)

2. *Appreciation*

Appreciation is a way of showing gratitude and thankfulness. Certainly, every human being feels good when appreciated, but women thrive on it more than men. Appreciation is another major marital expectation of a woman.

A simple appreciation is the dose a woman needs to go all the way. A woman can keep working without realizing she is tired when she is fondly appreciated. A word of appreciation is a powerful way to encourage anybody, especially a woman.

Many times, when a woman is working and she keeps passing by where the husband is seated, she is seriously trying to let the husband know that she needs some words of appreciation and encouragement. A wise and sensitive husband will not frustrate this marital expectation, but showers lots and lots of it on his wife.

Some words are very golden in life and in marriage. One of them is "Thank You". Other golden words are: "I love you", "I'm sorry" and "I forgive you". Couples need to keep saying

The Main Cause Of Marital Conflicts And The Solution

these words to each other till death do them part. "Thank you my darling". "I must say a big 'thank you' to you. "Thanks". "Thank you very much". "Thank you my babe". Thanks and thanks and thanks! These two words: "Thank you" is a great way to show appreciation to your spouse, especially, your wife. The more she is appreciated, the more she does for you and your kids. Don't take each other for granted. Many times, we are quicker to say 'thank you' to outsiders when they do any little favour, but we take our spouses for granted when they do the same things for us. Women thrive on appreciation more than men. Appreciation is a major marital need of a woman. She expects her husband to meet this need. So, she expects her husband to say 'thank you' and show appreciation in so many other ways. Husbands, this is one of your duties.

Gifts are another way of saying: 'thank you'. The gift needs not be expensive. It's the gesture that matters. Of course, if you can afford an expensive gift, why not? It's not the cost of the gift that really matters but your thoughtfulness. Gifts show appreciation. Yes, there should be exchange of gifts during anniversaries, birthdays and special occasions, but gifts bought when she least expects it speaks louder. You can buy flowers, wrist-watch, hair band, chocolate, candies etc. You can also buy gifts she once expressed her desire to have. You may pretend not to have heard her, but keep it in mind and get

Other Major Marital Needs Of A Wife

the item for her as a gift to appreciate her.

Appreciation can also be in form of love notes, with poetic words of appreciation for all her efforts to keeping the home running, the children under control and her care for her lovely husband. Love notes are fantastic ways of communicating love and appreciation.

Take your wife out for a dinner as a means of appreciating her. Tell her you don't want her to go through the trouble of cooking tonight. You want her to sit down in a nice environment and be served. This means you appreciate all her efforts in the kitchen.

Help her with chores at home. Don't watch her doing all the household chores while you cross your legs watching the TV. Assist her when you are at home especially on weekends. Let her feel your input, and then she believes you appreciate all her efforts for your assistance. You may just feel like helping to do the laundry, but it conveys a message of appreciation and a sense of worth to her. So, do it more because of the good message it conveys to her.

Researchers say 'touching' produces 'oxytocin', a hormone that diminishes stress and increases confidence. So, while

The Main Cause Of Marital Conflicts And The Solution

saying thank you, give her a hug. Put your hands around her shoulders and whisper a nice word of appreciation to her ears. Hold her hands. Kiss her. Touch her and say 'thank you".

Care for her health. Ephesians 5:28-29 says: "So ought men to love their wives as their own bodies. He that loves his wife loves himself. For no man ever yet hated his own flesh; but nourishes it, even as the Lord the church". When she is tired or ill, take a good care of her. Nourish her as you would your own body. Show understanding and be there for her when she can't get up to clean the house. Get up and do the cleaning. Ask her if she has taken her medications. If need be, drive her to the hospital. A woman can die for a caring man. She feels you appreciate her worth when you care for her.

When a man appreciates his wife, she feels recognized and important. Men also feel good when appreciated by their wives, but women thrive on it.

3. Security
Every woman seeks for security from her husband. To be secure means to be protected from danger or risk. One of the reasons God gave man a tough physiology is for the purpose of protecting their wife.

Other Major Marital Needs Of A Wife

However, there are two types of security. The first has to do with self confidence. This is when a woman is happy with herself and has a good self esteem. Much of this can be attributed to how she was raised and who brought her up. Insecure people usually externalize their feelings and blame people around them for their feelings. Insecure people usually read negative meanings to everything. They always believe everybody is attacking them, nobody loves them and that things are not always going their ways. No amount of efforts given to a woman who lacks self confidence will ever be sufficient to make her happy. The way to overcome this is to first identify the problem. This calls for an honest reality check. However, it is observed that finding peace and security with God is the surest way. The woman or the insecure man should first make a commitment of his/her life to Christ and through the study of God's word, find peace, love and security in God. Thereafter, she can start working on her self confidence, knowing that her happiness is not dependent on others but on her, with God's help and inspiration.

The story is told of a Samaritan woman in John 4. She was moving from one husband to the other, but still was thirsty for love, peace and acceptance. She was looking for what only God can give her in men. She was never satisfied with any of the men and was being passed around. However, when Jesus

The Main Cause Of Marital Conflicts And The Solution

met her and the missing link between her and God was restored, her countenance changed. She became joyful and happy. She left her waterpot and ran into the city to bring the whole city to Jesus. The joy of salvation is tremendous!

When David repented from his sin, he cried to God for the restoration of his Joy of salvation:
> *"Create in me a clean heart, o God; and*
> *renew a right spirit within me".*
> *Cast me not away from thy presence;*
> *and take not thy Holy Spirit from me.*
> *Restore unto me the joy of thy salvation;*
> *and uphold me with thy free spirit"*
> *(Psalm 51:50-12)*

It is difficult for a woman who is struggling with insecurity to feel loved and accepted by others. A woman who has always been talked down and called names while growing up will find it hard to believe it is real and that her husband means it when he says nice words to her. It will take some time for her after finding her bearing with God to completely come out of her world of insecurity. An understanding, matured and knowledgeable husband will be patient with her and see her through the process of reclaiming her self confidence. If such a woman could not find her bearing with God, it will take a longer time and with much more difficulties for her to

Other Major Marital Needs Of A Wife

rediscover herself in a right way, if at all.

The second type of security is the one a woman gets through her relationship with her husband in her marriage. She has a need to feel secure with her husband. This depends largely on whom her husband is and how her husband relates with her.

It is the responsibility of the man to provide for the needs of his family. A woman wants to be fully secured and assured that the husband is capable of meeting up with the financial needs of the family. When he is capable of meeting his family's financial needs, the wife feels secured. Money brings comfort. Every woman dreams of a very comfortable life in her marriage. Hence, the provision of money is very important to her. She can buy whatever she needs, drive a nice car, live in a comfortable accommodation, pay her bills, maintain her good look and enjoy her marriage. When the finance is not flowing, she is easily on the edge. When the money is flowing, she is restful and confident that bills are going to be paid and groceries are going to be bought. Every man should do his best and work hard to provide for his family. It will take a supernatural woman to still respect her husband when she is the one paying the bills. The natural woman will effectively rob it in. This usually leads to serious conflicts in marriage relationships. Money is very important

The Main Cause Of Marital Conflicts And The Solution

to a woman, even though, money is not all a woman needs to feel secure in her marriage. Marriages of the super rich also break down.

A woman needs a man that can lead and knows where he is going. She feels secure with a man that is in charge, who can set goals, give direction and lead from the front. A proactive man who takes initiatives. A leader who leads courageously and confidently. A leader who protects his family from external aggressions. Not a man who asks his wife to go and check out the noise in the middle of the night, but a man who makes good use of his strength and muscles to provide security for his household. Women need to be sure they are protected and well secured from external aggressions. That is why they always want their husbands to be around them especially at nights. A woman feels more secured when the husband is at home. Men should strive to always be there for their wives.

A woman also feels secure with a man who can hear God, lead his family in worship and be an example of a believer to his children. A man who can show his family the way of the Lord and he is leading his family to follow God. A man of integrity who is trustworthy can really make his wife fell secure. A man of his word, someone who does not tell lies or cheats, a man of

Other Major Marital Needs Of A Wife

character who is consistent in his ways, a man that is open, honest, predictable and has nothing to hide. A man whom his wife can rely on his words, if he says he is going somewhere, he would be found there.

A man with a listening ear! A woman feels secure with such a man. She needs someone she can confidently pour her heart into, who will give her a listening ear and not shout on her or put her down. She wants a man who shows understanding and proffers solution to her worries. A man whose words are seasoned with salt and he is compassionate. She seriously needs her husband to take her words seriously. A man who will close his newspaper or switch off the TV to hear her talk. She has to talk and her husband must listen! "In fact, the complaint from women that 'men don't listen tops almost every chart of women's grievances"[2]. She is secure when she knows she is very important to her husband. Next to God, she wants to be number one in the heart of her husband.

She is secure when she believes there is a future for her in her marriage. This happens when she sees that her husband is committed to the relationship and making future plans with her in the picture. She feels secure when her husband consults her before taking decisions, especially, major decisions for the family. She feels she is a part of the relationship when her

The Main Cause Of Marital Conflicts And The Solution

views are heard.

She also feels secure with a man that is matured and gifted in wisdom and understanding. She desires a man who can understand her and stand by her. A man who can handle her and support her emotionally. A man who loves her unconditionally and is satisfied with her. A man who is not a flirt.

Once a woman feels secure in her marriage, she is no longer on the edge. The fear of the unknown is reduced to the barest minimum. She becomes restful, hopeful and excited. She no longer reads meaning to every statement made and steps taken by her husband. In fact, her blood pressure no longer runs wild! A life committed to Christ helps a man to be a man of integrity and have a solid character. That is all she needs to have her need for security met.

Men are responsible for defending their wives before their family members. A woman needs a man that can talk for her before his parents.

4. *Family Commitment*
Every woman dreams of a husband that will be committed to her and their children. Women expect to see their husbands also involved in the caring and keeping of the home. Absentee

Other Major Marital Needs Of A Wife

husbands can never make good husbands or fathers.

A woman expects her husband to be there to discipline the children. There is a level of discipline that only the father can administer effectively. The father's 'baritone' voice alone is enough to send shivers down the spine of a naughty child. She also expects her husband to take the whole family out on picnics, sightseeing, for lunch or dinner, driving to the next city to see a family friend, etc.

When couples are newly married, they have all the time for each other. Not so long, children start coming into the picture. As soon as the children start arriving, part of their time and attention would be diverted to care for their children. The wife wants to see that her husband love their kids and care for them as much as he cares for her. She does not want to be left to carry the burden of the children alone. She wants to see her husband share in the burden and take the lead!

She needs him to set moral standard and see to the educational development of the children. She would be a happy woman when she sees him assisting the children with their homework. She wants to see him spend quality time with her and the children. This shows her that he is committed to the family.

The Main Cause Of Marital Conflicts And The Solution

A woman also wants to see her husband shelve other personal engagements to attend to school activities of their children like sports, play, PTA meetings e.t.c.

Women are easily committed to their families and they expect their husbands to get committed to the family too. When a man is nonchalant to this marital expectation of his wife, his wife becomes frustrated and unfulfilled in the marriage over time. Many women are just patching it up with the excuses of their husbands in this area. They are not enjoying it at all, and it's not funny to them! A sensitive and loving man will strive to meet up to his wife's legitimate marital expectations in order to have a fulfilled woman as a wife.

6
OTHER MAJOR MARITAL NEEDS OF A HUSBAND

Other major marital expectations of a husband are:

Physical attractiveness
Recreational companionship
Domestic support
Admiration.

1. Physical Attractiveness

Men and women are significantly different in so many ways. A man can easily be moved sexually by sight, while a woman is moved sexually by touch. Physical attractiveness is one

Other Major Marital Needs Of A Husband

strong factor that draws the heart and body of a man towards a woman. So, a man expects his wife to be physically attractive to him at all times.

A woman needs to make herself presentable to her husband. Women should watch how they look. Wise women know how to turn-on their husbands especially in the bedroom. A woman who refuses to keep herself tidy, beautiful and in shape can easily repulse any man.

Every wife should aspire to fulfil this marital need in her husband by looking after her dressing, hair style and weight. If you don't do your best to make yourself attractive to your husband, there are others outside who are working assiduously on themselves and parading themselves around your husband daily. Every wife knows what her husband wants and how he wants her to look. Please, always dress to please your husband.

However, women should not dress in such a way as to turn every man that sees them on the streets on sexually. They should please reserve their nudity for their husbands. Simple women are those who dress for everybody on the streets. Wives dress for themselves and for their husbands.

Men place value on beauty in selecting a wife. Women on the

The Main Cause Of Marital Conflicts And The Solution

other hand just want a caring and supportive man. Women love handsome men too, but beauty is not as important to women as it is to men in deciding whom to marry. Women should therefore understand that after marriage, the man still want her to look very beautiful. Many women out of the need to care for the home, the husband and the children don't have time to attend to their look any longer. This should not be so. A woman should not lose her dress sense after marriage. Trends, fashion, styles, cosmetics and fragrances are still very relevant in marriage. Exercising and/or dieting are also good to keep a woman in shape.

A woman should work on her beauty from inside to outside. Both are very important. A Christian woman should however, lay more emphasis on her inner beauty. Peter admonished Christian women in I Peter 3:3-4 to be adorned with the ornament of a meek and quiet spirit which is in the sight of God of a great price:

> *"Whose adorning let it not be that outward adorning of plaiting the hair, and of wearing of gold, or of putting on of apparel; But let it be the hidden man of the heart, in that which is not corruptible, even the ornament of a meek and quiet spirit, which is in the sight*

Other Major Marital Needs Of A Husband

of God of great price"

This means a Christian woman is to be adorned beautifully from the inside, much more importantly, then the outside. A woman is not to abandon outward beauty, but she who lays much effort on outward beauty to the detriment of her inner beauty has fallen short of God's standard. It does not mean that a woman should not adorn herself outwardly as some people believe. The outward beauty is important too. In fact, the inner beauty makes the outward beauty to be appreciated.

Some people use this passage to teach that women should not plait their hair or use jewelleries at all, that Christian women should only focus on their inner beauty and develop their character. This is far from being the truth. Peter spoke about three things: plaiting of hair, using of gold and putting on of apparel. It's surprising that they only pick two out of the three items to make up their prohibition list. If Peter was saying those three items should not be used, then it means that Christian women should not plait their hair, use gold or wear dresses at all. They should go about naked to prove their 'inner beauty'! Of course, no one can sensibly ask women to come to church naked to show their spirituality, that is why they pick only two items and leaves out the third. If that verse is a prohibitive list, then every item should fall under

The Main Cause Of Marital Conflicts And The Solution

prohibition. However, if only one item on the list cannot be prohibited, then, the others are not to be prohibited too.

The admonition of the Apostle Peter is instructive on where to lay more emphasis. A Christian woman should plait her hair, style her hair, care for her hair and look decent and neat. She should adorn herself with jewelleries moderately to enhance her beauty if she so desires, just as the plaiting of her hair enhances her beauty. She should also put on nice dresses. Moderation is what is needed here. The meat of the message is that a Christian woman should spend quality time to work on her character and let it be that people will see her for her godly virtues. A Christian woman should not be gorgeous outside and look unkempt inside. She should be moderately gorgeous outside and superlatively gorgeous inside.

2. *Recreational Companionship*

Recreational companionship is a good relationship builder. It helps couples to spend time together outside their normal routine of work and family. Men love sports. There is hardly any man who is not in love with one particular sport or the other. As a result of this, men expect to have a wife who will also love what they love. On the other hand, only a few women are really in love with sports. Men expect their wives to be a recreational companion and enjoy sports with them.

Other Major Marital Needs Of A Husband

Women should know that the love for sport is in-built in men. Once in a while, a wife should endeavour to accompany her husband on sporting outings as a means of her fulfilling her husband's marital expectations in this area.

During courtship, women don't have much problem accompanying their partners to watch football matches. After marriage, so many other things call for the attention of the wife and she is no longer interested in accompanying her husband on sporting activities. Some wives would rather have their husband join them in sporting activities they prefer or ask him to go on with his sporting activities without them. Doing sports together creates more bonding between husband and wife. Couples can sit down and agree on sports they can do together either weekly or monthly. It will do a lot of good to their marriage and fulfil an important need on the list of the husband.

Recreational activities are not limited to sports. Watching interesting TV programs together or going to the cinema, attending church services together and regularly, eating out, attending seminars/conferences, going on camping and retreats also count as recreational activities. The important thing is to be together in an indoor or outdoor activity that you both enjoy. This is an opportunity for couples to be in a

The Main Cause Of Marital Conflicts And The Solution

relaxed atmosphere and enjoy something together for a period of time regularly before they move back into the family routines.

In a Christian setup, attending church activities together, listening to sermons, going out on church outreaches, praying together and growing in faith under the same spiritual atmosphere contribute greatly to marital peace and harmony. This is a great opportunity Christians should avail themselves of to grow spiritually and together in their marriage. What a great opportunity that makes a lot of difference!

3. *Domestic Support*

Naturally, women are home makers. God made them so because men are generally lacking in such details. Most bachelors look forward to a day when they won't have to bother so much about cooking, washing and cleaning. Even though, a bachelor will do all these while not yet married, as soon as he is married, he suddenly becomes 'lazy' and leaves all the chores for his wife. He naturally expects his wife to take over from where he stopped.

God made the woman a caring personality. As soon as a woman gets married, she naturally takes over the kitchen and the responsibilities of cleaning the house. As soon as the

Other Major Marital Needs Of A Husband

children start arriving, she also devotes much of her time to caring for them. When a man sees his wife cooking his meals, cleaning the house, ironing his clothes and taking a good care of the children, he is convinced that his wife really loves him.

Men should also give a helping hand to their wives at home. The house work is actually the man's job. A woman is a helpmeet. She was created by God to help the man. Men should not become insensitive to an extent that they don't know when to assist at home. When a woman is overworked and tired, her best can no longer come out in other things.

One big problem a working mother faces is how to meet her husband's marital expectation of giving him enough domestic support. Many homes therefore become un-kept and disorganized. The children are not well supervised and every time, the dinner is late. It is not healthy for the family, if husband and wife close late from work. Some women are also over pampered by their parents such that they know next to nothing about keeping the home and cooking a nice meal. House maids cannot do everything a wife needs to know how to do. A man necessarily wants to see his wife's touch in the home.

Giving domestic support means so much to a man. It is a way for a wife to tell her husband 'I love you and care for you", 'I

The Main Cause Of Marital Conflicts And The Solution

am yours, always at your service'. A man who cannot get good food to eat at home will always eat outside. Men love good and tasty food. Women should do their best to provide sufficient domestic support for their husbands and thereby, make them eager to always return home.

4. Admiration

'Admiration' is a feeling of pleasure and respect[3]. To be respected is a marital expectation of a man. No man dreams of marrying a wife who won't respect him. A woman greatly needs her husband to appreciate her while a man needs his wife to admire him.

It destabilizes a man's emotions when his wife addresses him without any respect. He also expects his wife to commend the way he is working hard to care for the family. When a man had been shouted upon in the office or even queried, he expects to make up for the drop in his self esteem at home by the admiration of his wife. He wants his wife to tell him how important and hard working he is. When he arrives home, he expects his wife to welcome him with a smile, collect his briefcase and offer him a glass of cold water. Women who don't know how to receive their husbands warmly into the house after a day's work drive them out. That is why some men take to bad habits like smoking and drinking because they don't have a warm home to return to. A wise woman will

Other Major Marital Needs Of A Husband

do her best to meet the admiration need of her husband in order to play her part in keeping her home together.

7
YOU CAN MAKE IT

"I can do all things through Christ which strengtheneth me" (Phil. 4:13)

The list of marital expectations of both husband and wife is inexhaustible. Those ones we have considered are the marital needs or expectations that are generally considered to be the major ones. Efforts must be taken by couples to meet these major needs. Also find out other things your spouse expects from you as a marriage partner and plot ways of meeting such needs. Remember, it is your responsibility to give yourself to doing those things that will make your marriage work before your marriage can work.

You Can Make It

You can do it! Your marriage can succeed. You can give your wife quality time for sharing, since it is for the benefit of your marriage. You can both start improving on your sexual fellowship. You can season your words with salt before saying them to your spouse. No matter how 'terrible' and 'uncooperative' your spouse seems to be, you can decide to make a difference from your own end and trust God for your spouse to catch up with you.

I can do all things through Christ! When couples are in Christ, they receive strength from Christ to do all things they desire to do. That kind of strength they receive from Christ cannot be accessed anywhere else.

Salvation through Christ brings inner peace and harmony. This is the strength we need to do all things in this life. When you are at peace with God, then you can be at peace with yourself and others. If you have not found peace with God, you will be looking for it in others or in things and you easily get frustrated and discouraged because it becomes elusive. *"Peace I leave with you, my peace I give unto you: not as the world giveth, give I unto you. Let not your heart be troubled, neither let it be afraid"* (John 14:27)

Jesus gives peace. A couple who are in Christ can be helped by

The Main Cause Of Marital Conflicts And The Solution

God to overcome obstacles in life. If you are still strong on the inside, you can keep going on the outside. Once you lose the battle on the inside, you fall on the outside. Successful marriage is possible for you. Discover it, believe it and do it. You can make it.

Write to tell me your testimonies.

References

[1] Willard F. Harley, "His Needs Her Needs" Monarch Books Oxford, UK.

[2] www.yourtango.com/2015283064/secret-getting-men-listen-you

[3] Longman's Dictionary of English

Contact:

www.remioluyale.com
Email: info@remioluyale.com
Tel: +234 802 305 9599
Whatsapp: +2348023059599
Twitter: @remioluyale
Https://www.facebook.com/oluremi.oluyale

www.ingramcontent.com/pod-product-compliance
Lightning Source LLC
Chambersburg PA
CBHW061339040426
42444CB00011B/2998